- All information s purpose only and us the responsibility for using it.

- Although I took tremendous effort to ensure that all information provided in this guide are correct, I will welcome your suggestions if you find out that any information provided in this guide is inadequate or you find a better way of doing some of the actions mentioned in this guide. All correspondence should be sent to pharmibrahimguides@gmail.com

Copyright and Trademarks

Power Pressure Cooker XL is a trademark of Tristar Products, Inc. All other trademarks are the property of their respective owners. Reproduction of this book without the permission of the owner is illegal. Any request for permission should be directed to pharmibrahimguides@gmail.com.

Copyright © 2017 by Pharm Ibrahim

About This Guide

Finally, a straightforward and succinct cookbook and manual on Power Pressure Cooker XL for newbies, seniors, students, instructors and homemakers is here. This is the guide that should have been included in the box.

I know you have a lot of things to do and you will not want to be bothered by irrelevant things, so I have made this manual/cookbook to be straightforward. Interestingly, it is a step-by-step manual so you can be confident that you will understand the information contained inside it.

In addition, this cookbook contains 30-day Power Pressure Cooker XL meal plan that will introduce you to different varieties of food you can make with your pressure cooker. And guess what? Many of these recipes are simple to make and are healthy.

PS: Please make sure you don't give the gift of Power Pressure Cooker XL without given this companion guide alongside with it. This guide makes your gift a complete one.

Table of Contents

How to Use This Guide   vi

How Does Pressure Cooking Work?   1

Get to know your pressure cooker   2

   Device Layout of Power Pressure Cooker XL (showing The Buttons and the Digital Surface)   2

   Device Layout of Power Pressure Cooker XL (showing The Handle and surface)   7

Turning your Power Pressure Cooker XL on and off   8

Getting started with Power Pressure Cooker XL   8

More about the Pressure Valve   13

Removing and Inserting the Float Valve   14

More about the Inner Pot   16

Cooking Different Types of Food with Power Pressure Cooker XL   18

   General instructions on using Power Pressure Cooker   18

   Sautéing Vegetable   21

   Frying Food Items Using Power Pressure Cooker XL   23

   Using "Slow Cook" In Power Pressure Cooker XL   23

   Boiling Egg Using Power Pressure Cooker XL   24

   Cooking Frozen Food Using Power Pressure Cooker XL   25

   Special Notes on Cooking Rice, Beans and Other Food That Expand During Cooking   26

Where to Get Good Recipes to Cook on Power Pressure Cooker   27

Cleaning Power Pressure Cooker XL   28

Disadvantages of Power Pressure Cooker XL   29

Troubleshooting Power Pressure Cooker XL   29

30-Day Power Pressure Cooker XL Meal Plan — an Executive Guide to Different Varieties of Food You Can Make with Your Pressure Cooker   32

    Day 1 – Spinach and Mushroom Frittata   36

    Day 2 – Honey Cinnamon Steel-Cut Oats   38

    Day 3 – Sausage and Egg Casserole   39

    Day 4 – Sweet Raspberry Jam   42

    Day 5 – Creamy Maple Apple Oatmeal   44

    Day 6 – Chocolate Berry Breakfast Cake   46

    Day 7 – Tomato Basil Frittata   49

    Day 8 – Cinnamon Baked French Toast   51

    Day 9 – Hearty Beef and Red Bean Chili   53

    Day 10 – Split Pea and Smoked Turkey Soup   55

    Day 11 – Beef and Vegetable Stew   57

    Day 12 – New England Clam Chowder   60

    Day 13 – Herbed Butternut Squash Soup   62

    Day 14 – Lentil and Carrot Soup   64

    Day 15 – Squash, Spinach and White Bean Soup   66

    Day 16 – Beef and Mushroom Stroganoff   69

    Day 17 – Braised Lamb Shanks   72

    Day 18 – Raspberry Glazed Chicken   75

    Day 19 – Creamy Mushroom Risotto   77

    Day 20 – Easy Chicken Cacciatore   79

    Day 21 – Beef Burgundy with Egg Noodles   81

    Day 22 – Vegan Chickpea Curry   83

Day 23 – Corned Beef and Cabbage	85
Day 24 – Chocolate Coconut Rice Pudding	87
Day 25 – Easy Baked Apples	89
Day 26 – Chocolate Cookie Cheesecake	91
Day 27 – Vanilla Poached Pears	94
Day 28 – Raspberry Raisin Bread Pudding	96
Day 29 – Fluffy Chocolate Cake	98
Day 30 – Lemon Cheesecake with Berries	100

Just Before You Go…(Please Read!)   **103**

How to Use This Guide

This guide is an unofficial manual/cookbook of Power Pressure Cooker XL and it should be used just like you use any reference book or manual.

To quickly find a topic, please use the table of contents. In addition, you can press **Ctrl + F** if you are using a PC, if not press the menu icon (usually located at the right top corner of the screen) of your reading app and select **"Search"** to search for any phrase in this guide. Searching for keywords or phrase will allow you to quickly find information and save time.

I hope this guide helps you get the most out of your Power Pressure Cooker XL.

How Does Pressure Cooking Work?

If you are using a pressure cooker for the first time, you may not know how pressure cooking works. Pressure cooking involves cooking food in a sealed container and thereby preventing escape of steam. This sealed container is commonly referred to as pressure cooker.

Pressure cooking works on the principle that in a sealed vessel temperature increases with increase in pressure. The increase in pressure is created by the trapped steam inside a pressure cooker (don't forget that pressure can be simply defined as physical force exerted on or against an object by something in contact with it). Cooking your food under pressure allows you to cook it faster.

Get to know your pressure cooker

Device Layout of Power Pressure Cooker XL (showing The Buttons and the Digital Surface)

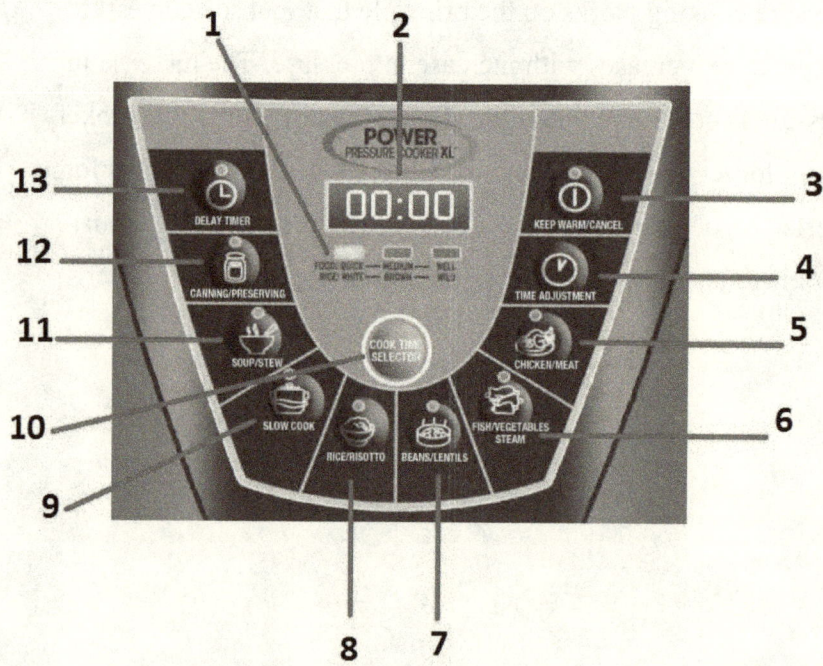

Number	Function
1.	LED Display: This display changes to indicate the type or status of food you are cooking. For example, if you are cooking white rice and you have selected the RICE button, the white LED will turn on.
2.	LED Display for Time: This display shows the time it is going to take to get your food cooked. The LED Display will show four zeros (0000) when first plugged in. The four zeros will change to a default time when you press any cooking button such as SOUP/STEW button. The default time will appear for few seconds and then the LED Display will begin to rotate. The rotation signifies that the pressure cooker is building up pressure. The pressure building process usually takes some time (it can take up to 17 minutes). Once the required pressure is built, the rotating process will stop and the pressure cooker will begin counting down the time. When the countdown is completed the pressure cooker will make a small sound and automatically enter the KEEP WARM mode.
3.	KEEP WARM/CANCEL: Press this button to cancel any cooking process. If you are cooking and you remember that you have forgotten to add an

ingredient (e.g. salt), just press the KEEP WARM/CANCEL button and then carefully rotate the Pressure Valve (using an object like knife or long fork) to the OPEN position. Then wait for the pressure to be released and carefully turn the handle clockwise to open. Make sure the lid is opened away from you to be on a safer side. When the pressure cooker is in KEEP WARM mode, pressing the KEEP WARM/CANCEL should cancel the KEEP WARM process.

4. TIME ADJUSTMENT: Press this button to adjust the time as you like. The TIME ADJUSTMENT button allows you to customize the amount of time your food is going to spend cooking. You may use this button to set your preferred time.

Downside: It appears that you may only be able to increase the cooking time using the TIME ADJUSTMENT button, you may not be able to reduce the time (minutes) using this button. If you need to reduce the minutes your food is going to spend cooking after you have set a higher time, press the KEEP WARM/CANCEL button and then press a food button corresponding to the time you want to cook. If you need to increase the cook time, press the TIME ADJUSTMENT button.

Tip: If you want to cook your food for a very small

	time, press FISH/VEGETABLES/STEAM button. This button gives you 2 minutes cook time by default. If you need more time press the TIME ADJUSTMENT button.
5.	CKICKEN/MEAT: Press this button if you are cooking meat or chicken.
6.	FISH/VEGETABLES/STEAM: Press this button if you are cooking fish or vegetables.
7.	BEANS/LENTILS: Press this button if you are cooking beans or lentils.
8.	RICE/RISOTTO: Press this button if you are cooking rice or risotto.
9.	SLOW COOK: Press this button if you want to slow cook your food for several hours
10.	COOK TIME SELECTOR: Use this button to adjust the default time for a specific food program. For example, when you press the SLOW COOK button, the default time is 2 hours, but you can use the COOK TIME SELECTOR button to adjust it to 6 hours or 12 hours. Also you can use COOK TIME SELECTOR button to select the preferred program for White, Brown or Wild rice.
11.	SOUP/STEW: Press this button if you are cooking soup or stew.
12.	CANNING/PRESERVING: Press this button to start a canning or preserving program. Canning is a

	method of preserving a food substance.
13.	DELAY TIMER: This button allows you to cook your food at a convenient time. Delay Timer allows your food to cook at a later time (up to 24 hours).

Downside: There is no minus button to reduce the time you have selected. You have to select the button with closest time and then use the TIME ADJUSTMENT button to add up time.

Device Layout of Power Pressure Cooker XL (showing The Handle and surface)

Number	Function
1.	Pressure Cooker Lid Handle
2.	Pressure Release Valve/Pressure Valve
3.	Stainless Steel Body (containing the inner pot)
4.	Power Pressure Cooker XL Base
5.	Control Buttons

6.	Pressure Cooker Digital Display
7.	Lock Controls Surface/Screen
8.	Safe Lock Lid

Turning your Power Pressure Cooker XL on and off

Just like many other pressure cookers, turning on your device is as simple as ABC. To turn on your Power Pressure Cooker XL, just connect it to a power output using the power adapter that came with it. The digital display on Power Pressure Cooker XL turns on showing four zeros.

To turn off Power Pressure Cooker XL, unplug it from the power source.

Tip: It is recommended to place your Power Pressure Cooker XL on a stable flat surface when using it.

Getting started with Power Pressure Cooker XL

You will need to clean and setup Power Pressure Cooker XL before you start using it. To clean Power Pressure Cooker XL:

1. Carefully unbox the Power Pressure Cooker XL product box using a sharp knife to cut the seals.
2. Carefully remove the Power Pressure Cooker XL and the accessories from the product box.

3. Remove the rubber gasket from the pressure lid using the Pull Tab located under the pressure lid. Make sure the **float valve** (see page 14) on the pressure lid does not get removed in the process.

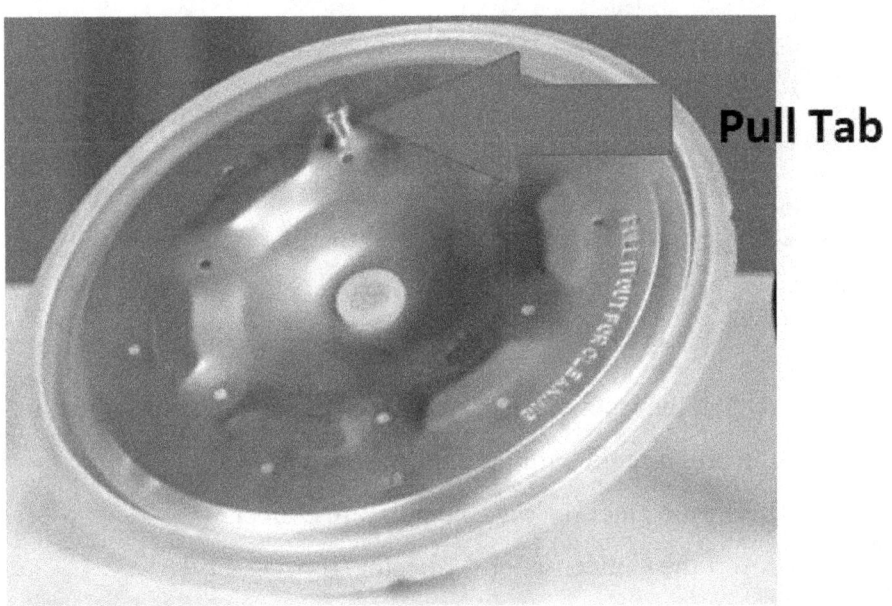

4. Then remove the Rubber Liner from the gasket.

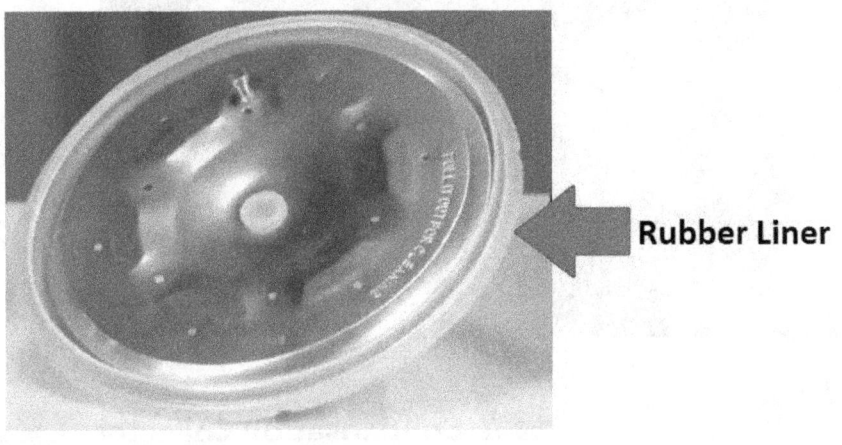

5. Clean the rubber gasket, the lid and the inner pot in soapy water and then rinse them in water. Then dry them.

Inner Pot

6. Attach the Rubber Liner to the gasket and then place them in the pressure lid until they fit/lock into place.
7. Insert the inner pot into the pressure cooker.
8. Insert the Condensation Collector (if necessary).

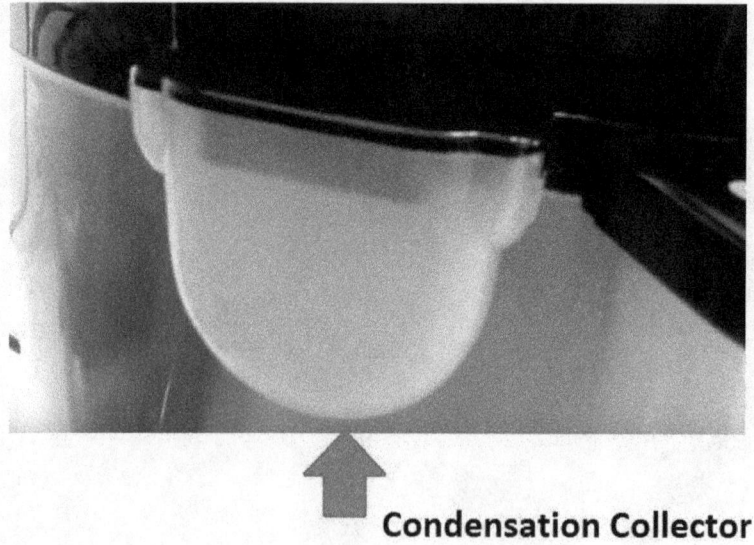
Condensation Collector

9. Connect one end of the power adapter to the Power Pressure Cooker XL and then connect the other end to a power source. It turns on automatically. There is no power button.

To ensure that the Rubber Gasket is lock into place, it is important you perform the following actions:
1. Fill the inner pot with water so that it is about two-third full.
2. Connect the Pressure Cooker to a power source as described above.
3. Close the pressure cooker with the pressure lid and rotate it to **Lock** position.

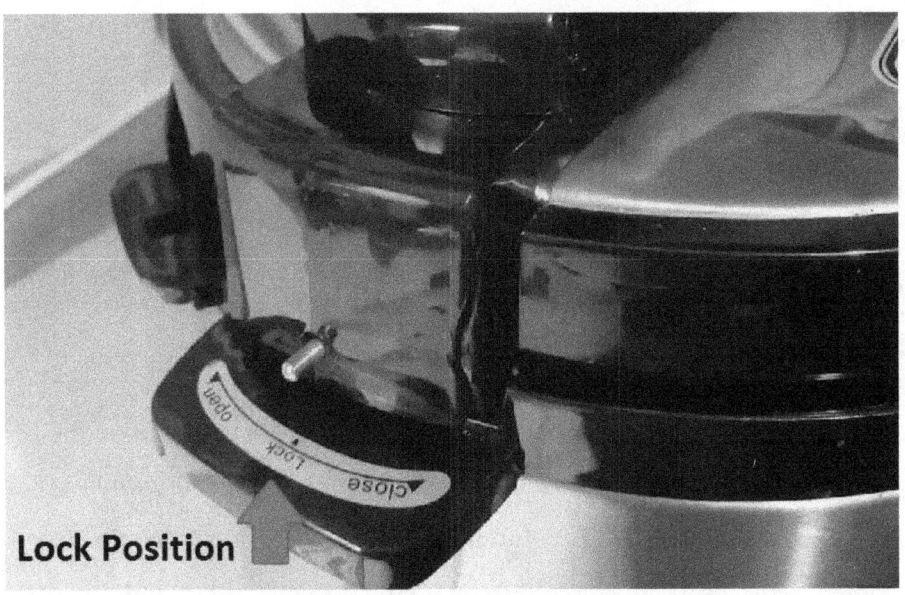
Lock Position

4. Rotate the Pressure Valve to seal position. The small triangle on the Valve must align with the triangle on the pressure lid.

11

This two must align

5. Press the CANNING/PRESERVING button and run it for ten minutes.
6. When the canning process is finished, use a fork or a stick to rotate the Pressure Valve to open position (see the picture below) and allow all the trapped pressure to escape.

Make sure these two are aligned.

I will advise you use a long fork/prong or stick to open the Pressure Valve so as to avoid burning your hand with hot steam coming out of the pressure cooker. Some people also prefer to put a small towel on the pressure valve, but this may be unnecessary since the steam gets cooler as it rises.

7. Allow the water inside the inner pot to cool to room temperature and then pour it away. The Rubber Gasket

should now fit into place and your Pressure Cooker is now ready for use.

Note:

When using Power Pressure Cooker XL, please ensure that the Pressure Valve is closed when you close the lid. However, you may leave the Pressure Valve open if you are using the Slow Cooking (see page 23) feature of the Power Pressure Cooker.

More about the Pressure Valve

The Pressure Valve allows you to prevent steam from escaping from the Power Pressure Cooker XL. When you are using the pressure cooker, you must always ensure that the Pressure Valve is properly closed (after closing the lid).

If you are using the Slow Cook feature, you may not bother to close the Pressure Valve. This is not required during Slow Cooking.

One of the disadvantages of Pressure Valve is that the mark on it may get removed after using it for some time. Another disadvantage is that the Pressure Valve rotates so easily and may become unstable occasionally. I would have loved something that is quite/slightly difficult to move.

Removing and Inserting the Float Valve

You might want to remove the float valve so as to do thorough cleaning of your pressure lid.

To remove the float valve:
1. Remove the rubber gasket from the pressure lid using the Pull Tab located under the pressure lid. This will expose the float valve under the pressure lid.

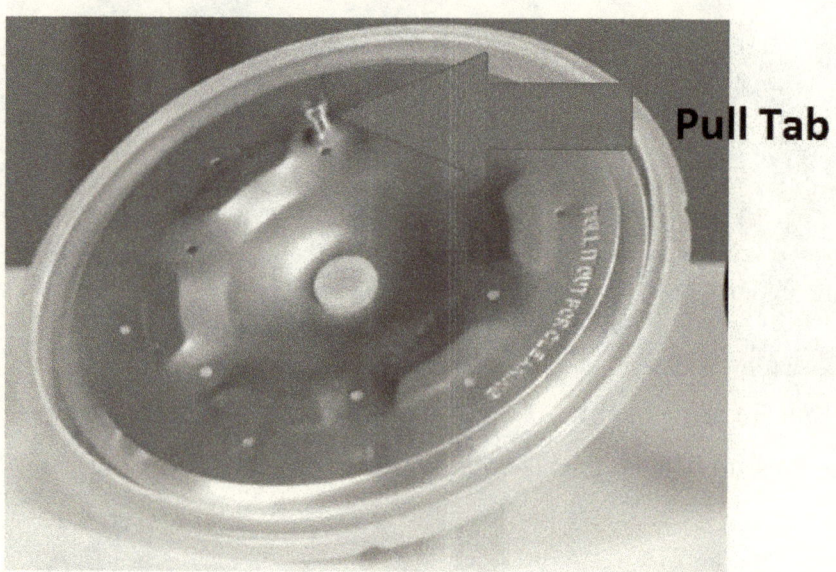

2. Carefully remove the small circular rubber piece on the float valve. The float valve should fall after removing the rubber piece.

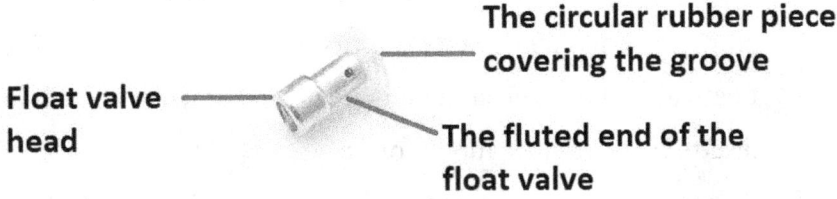

Float valve head — The circular rubber piece covering the groove

The fluted end of the float valve

To insert the float valve:
1. Pick up the float valve and remove the circular rubber piece (if necessary).
2. Drop float valve inside the hole on the pressure lid. Making sure the side with groove is facing down and the head is facing up (see the picture above).

The hole inside the Pressure Lid

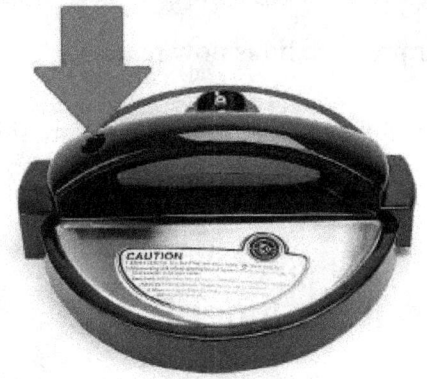

3. Insert a slim object (e.g. pencil) into the hole on the pressure lid so as to press the head of the float valve. This will make the fluted end of the float valve to stick out.
4. Carefully placed the circular rubber piece onto the fluted end of the float valve. Make sure the circular rubber piece sits properly on the groove (see the first picture on page 15). The float valve should be able to move up and down after inserting the circular rubber piece.
5. Place the rubber gasket inside the pressure lid until it fit/lock into place.

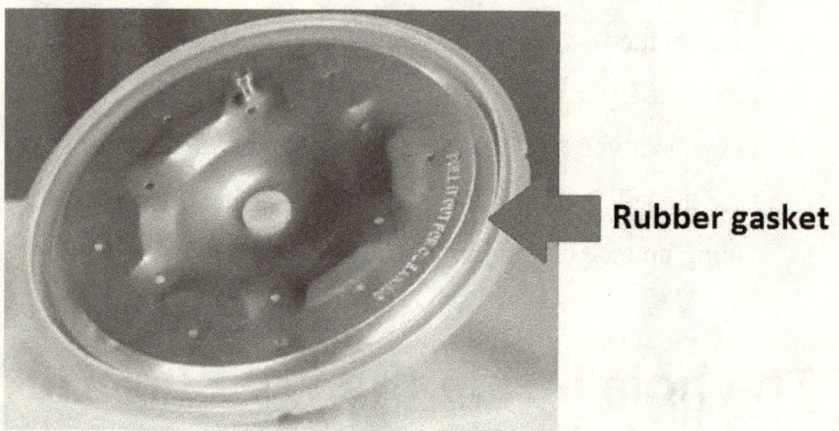

← Rubber gasket

6. Your pressure lid is now ready for usage.

Tip: Be careful when washing the pressure lid so that the float valve does not get removed unintentionally.

More about the Inner Pot

The inner pot is the container that will be holding your food during the cooking process.

# Inner Pot

You must ensure that you don't fill the inner pot more than the maximum limit indicated on the inside of the pot.

One of the disadvantages of the inner pot is that it may become more difficult to clean after some time. You will probably love the beautiful nature of this pot when you start using it but please know that this love of yours may be short-lived.

Cooking Different Types of Food with Power Pressure Cooker XL

General instructions on using Power Pressure Cooker

There are some general steps to follow when using the Power Pressure Cooker XL. The steps are discussed below:

Please note that I assumed you have already prepared your Power Pressure Cooker XL for use following the steps mentioned on page 8.

1. Get ready the food items you want to cook.
2. Connect the pressure cooker to the power source. The Power Pressure Cooker then powers on automatically. There is no power button.
3. Press an appropriate cook button. If you want to sauté or fry some food items before you add (other) food ingredients, you can press the CHICKEN/MEAT button (there is no browning or sauté button), wait for a minute or two for the pressure cooker to heat up and then start frying your food items. After you are done, press the KEEP WARM/CANCEL button.

In addition, you may use the COOK TIME SELECTOR or TIME ADJUSTMENT button to customize your cook time as you like.

4. Put all (other) ingredients into the inner pot and add appropriate amount of liquid (e.g. water, broth etc.).
5. Close the pressure cooker with the pressure lid.
6. Press an appropriate cook button. If you are cooking soup, press the SOUP button.
7. The default time will appear for few seconds and then the LED Display will begin rotating. The rotation signifies the pressure cooker is building up pressure. The pressure building process usually takes some time (up to 17 minutes). Once the required pressure is built, the rotating process will stop and the pressure cooker will begin counting down the time.
8. Rotate the Pressure Valve to **Lock** position. The small triangle on the Valve must align with the triangle on the lid.
9. After the time countdown, the Power Pressure Cooker will make a small sound and automatically enter the KEEP WARM mode. The Power Pressure Cooker XL can keep your food in KEEP WARM mode for up to four hours. Please note that your food may lose its good flavor if it takes too long in KEEP WARM mode. I will advise you don't allow your food to spend more than four hours in KEEP WARM mode.
10. When the cooking process is finished (after the cooking time has elapsed), use a long fork or a stick to rotate the Pressure

Valve to open position (see the picture below) and allow all the trapped pressure to escape.

Make sure these two are aligned.

I will advise you use a long fork/prong or stick to open the Pressure Valve so as to avoid burning your hand with hot steam coming out of the pressure cooker. Some people also prefer to put a small towel on the pressure valve, but this may be unnecessary since the steam gets cooler as it rises.

11. Open the lid after the pressure finish escaping (this may take some seconds/minutes).
12. Serve your food and enjoy!

Tip: You can use Power Pressure Cooker XL just like you use your electric cooker and traditional pot. To do this, just replace the Power Pressure Cooker XL lid with a glass lid. You can buy a glass lid from Amazon. In addition, you may leave the Pressure Valve open if you don't have a glass lid.

Notes:

- After closing the pressure cooker with the lid, you may notice that a little amount of steam is coming out of the top or side of the pressure cooker. If this happens then make sure the pressure lid is properly seated and locked. In addition, if you have tampered with the float valve (if you have disassembled it), make sure you properly assembled it by following the steps on page 14/15.
  However, please note that it is normal for condensation to appear in condensation collector (even while the pressure valve is properly closed.)
- Avoid coming in contact with hot droppings from the pressure lid while removing it after finishing a cooking program.
- Make sure the Power Pressure Cooker XL's power cord does not come in contact with hot surface or liquid.

Sautéing Vegetable

Frying vegetables in vegetable oil like olive oil has been proven to be beneficial to our health. This is better than boiling vegetables in water.

To sauté your vegetables:
I will advise that you sauté your vegetables just like you do in normal pan.
1. Wash the vegetables in water (if necessary).

2. Cut your vegetables into bite-sized pieces so that they can get cooked easily.
3. Insert the inner pot into the Power Pressure Cooker (if necessary) and then connect the pressure cooker to the power source. The Power Pressure Cooker then powers on automatically. There is no power button.
4. Press the MEAT/CHICKEN button.
5. Put vegetable oil into the inner pot and wait until it begins to shimmer. It takes few minute(s). The quantity of oil you use depends on the quantity of vegetables you are cooking.
6. Add your vegetables and other desired ingredients and stir occasionally and they nicely brown and cooked through. Stirring the vegetables will make them cook evenly.
You may not need to close the pressure cooker with the pressure lid while sautéing your vegetables. If you must close the pressure cooker, then don't close the pressure valve or you may just close the pressure cooker with a glass lid (if you have one). The time the vegetables take to cook depends on the type of vegetables. It usually takes between 3 and 10 minutes. When you feel that the vegetable is cooked, just press the CANCEL/KEEP WARM button.
7. Turn off the Power Pressure Cooker XL and remove the inner pot to avoid over cooking your vegetables. Serve the vegetables and enjoy!

Tip: Right before the vegetables are done, you may add any seasonings you want. These may include pepper, salt etc.

Frying Food Items Using Power Pressure Cooker XL

You can use the Power Pressure Cooker XL to fry or brown food items. To do this, follow the steps mentioned under sautéing vegetables (see page 21/22). Just make sure you replace the vegetables with the food you want to brown/fry.

Using " Slow Cook" In Power Pressure Cooker XL

You can use slow cook feature in Power Pressure Cooker. This feature allows you to cook your food for a longer period of time. The default slow cook time is 2 hours but you can use the COOK TIME SELECTOR to adjust it to 6 or 12 hours.

When using the Slow Cook feature, please remember to use a glass lid as the cover for your pressure cooker. If you must use the Power Pressure Cooker XL's lid then you must leave the pressure valve open. In addition, if you don't have a glass lid, you can use a plate to cover the pressure cooker.

Boiling Egg Using Power Pressure Cooker XL

One of the smartest ways to boil eggs is to boil it in a pressure cooker. To do this:

1. Connect the pressure cooker to the power source. The Power Pressure Cooker then power on automatically. There is no power button.
2. Add a cup (or two cups) of water into the inner pot.
3. Put the steamer tray inside the inner pot making sure it sit properly. The steamer tray is hollow tray that came with your Power Pressure Cooker XL. Please note that you can also use a wire rack instead of steamer tray.
4. Put the eggs on the steamer tray.
5. Press the FISH/VEGETABLES/STEAM button and then use the TIME ADJUSTMENT button to increase the time to 6 minutes.
6. Close the lid.
7. Rotate the Pressure Valve to **Lock** position. The small triangle on the Valve must align with the triangle on the lid.
8. When the cooking process is finished (after the cooking time has elapsed), use a long fork or a stick to rotate the Pressure Valve to open position (see the picture below) and allow all the trapped pressure to escape.

Make sure these two are aligned.

9. Open the lid after the pressure finish escaping (this may take some seconds/minutes), remove the eggs and put them in water bath with ice cubes.
10. Peel your eggs and enjoy!

Cooking Frozen Food Using Power Pressure Cooker XL

You can use Power Pressure Cooker XL to cook frozen foods. You may not need to follow any special instructions when cooking frozen foods with Power Pressure Cooker XL, just follow the instructions on your recipe as you would when cooking unfrozen food. However, you may need to add few extra minutes to you cook time when cooking frozen food. For example, if you are cooking frozen meats, remember to add extra 10 minutes to your cook time. You can use the COOK TIME SELECTOR or TIME ADJUSTMENT button to customize the cook time as you like.

Special Notes on Cooking Rice, Beans and Other Food That Expand During Cooking

As a rule, you must not fill the inner pot above the halfway point when cooking rice, beans or other food item that expand during cooking process. Filling the cooking unit more than the halfway point may lead to development of excess pressure and this is usually unwanted.

Where to Get Good Recipes to Cook on Power Pressure Cooker

There are several hundreds of recipes out there that you can try out on your Power Pressure Cooker XL. There are many websites that provide free information on recipes. Personally, I like to visit educational websites for my recipe information. This is because educational websites give quality information.

To access recipes information contained on "edu" websites, just go to Google and type **site:.edu recipes for (mention a type of food).** In addition you may just type **site:.edu recipe.** You may also search for organizations providing recipe information by going to Google and typing **site:.org recipes for (mention a type of food).**

Please note that it is not necessary you follow every aspect of a recipe. You may decide to avoid some ingredient(s) mentioned in a recipe if you see that doing so is beneficial to you. No law says you must follow a recipe loyally. In fact, you may modify a recipe to your taste.

Just make sure you take healthy diets. For example, if I were you I would avoid trans fats, alcohol etc.

Cleaning Power Pressure Cooker XL

It is advisable to clean the Power Pressure Cooker XL after each cooking program. To do this:

1. Disconnect the Power Pressure Cooker XL from an electric source.
2. Allow Power Pressure Cooker XL to cool down (if necessary).
3. Remove the lid and inner pot.
4. Remove the rubber gasket for the pressure lid and clean both the lid and the rubber gasket using mild liquid detergent with a soft cloth or sponge. Please follow the instructions on page 9 to remove the rubber gasket from the lid.
5. Wash the inner pot with mild liquid detergent and a soft cloth or sponge.
6. Thoroughly rinse the lid, the rubber gasket and the inner pot in water and then dry them.
7. Using a damp cloth, clean the outer surface (containing the digital display).

Notes:

1. Don't use abrasive power, harsh washing detergent, scouring pads/powders, or bleaching agent to clean the Power Pressure Cooker XL. You should instead use mild liquid detergent with a soft cloth or sponge.

2. Don't pour water into the inner surface of the pressure cooker. The inner surface is the surface that remains after you remove the inner pot. If you need to clean inner surface, use a clean damp towel and make sure it has dried properly before you use the pressure cooker again.

Disadvantages of Power Pressure Cooker XL

The Power Pressure Cooker XL has few disadvantages. These disadvantages are mentioned below:
1. The inner pot gets darker easily. Even if you clean it every time, it is very likely that the inner pot will eventually get some stain that will be very difficult to remove.
2. The mark on the Power Pressure Cooker XL's pressure valve can get erased after using it for some time.
3. The steam collector can get lost easily.
4. There is no browning button.

Troubleshooting Power Pressure Cooker XL

Although much effort have been put into making this machine, it is possible that Power Pressure Cooker XL will misbehave at one time or the other. When this happen there are few things to do.

If steam is coming out from the top of the Power Pressure Cooker XL

- Ensure that the pressure valve is in lock position. The small triangle on the Valve must align with the triangle on the lid.

This two must align

- Ensure that the lid is properly closed and seated.
- Ensure that the rubber gasket (see page 9) is properly seated in the lid.

Water appear in the condensation collector

- Please note that it is normal for condensation to appear in condensation collector (even while the pressure valve is properly closed.)

The Power Pressure Cooker XL turns off automatically

- This may be caused by overheating. Unplug the pressure cooker from power source and allow the cooker to cool down for at least 30 minutes.
- If the cooker does not turn on after allowing it to rest, then contact the Power Pressure Cooker XL Customer Service on 1-973-287-5169.

Cannot Open the Lid of Power Pressure Cooker XL

- Ensure that all the trapped pressure has been released. This may take more than a minute.
- Ensure that nothing is blocking the pressure valve vent. Also ensure that the pressure valve is in open position. You may use a prong to push the pressure valve to open position.

Make sure these two are aligned.

30-Day Power Pressure Cooker XL Meal Plan — an Executive Guide to Different Varieties of Food You Can Make with Your Pressure Cooker

Power Pressure Cooker XL Recipes Include:

Spinach and Mushroom Frittata

Honey Cinnamon Steel-Cut Oats

Sausage and Egg Casserole

Sweet Raspberry Jam

Creamy Maple Apple Oatmeal

Chocolate Berry Breakfast Cake

Tomato Basil Frittata

Cinnamon Baked French Toast

Hearty Beef and Red Bean Chili

Split Pea and Smoked Turkey Soup

Beef and Vegetable Stew

New England Clam Chowder

Herbed Butternut Squash Soup

Lentil and Carrot Soup

Squash, Spinach and White Bean Soup

Beef and Mushroom Stroganoff

Braised Lamb Shanks

Raspberry Glazed Chicken

Creamy Mushroom Risotto

Easy Chicken Cacciatore

Beef Burgundy with Egg Noodles

Vegan Chickpea Curry

Corned Beef and Cabbage

Chocolate Coconut Rice Pudding

Easy Baked Apples

Chocolate Cookie Cheesecake

Vanilla Poached Pears

Raspberry Raisin Bread Pudding

Fluffy Chocolate Cake

Lemon Cheesecake with Berries

General Suggestions for the Completion of 30-Day Power Pressure Cooker XL Meal Plan

- You don't need to close the pressure cooker with the pressure lid while **sautéing** your food. If you must close the pressure cooker, then don't close the pressure valve or you may just close the pressure cooker with a glass lid (if you have one).
- You can use the TIME ADJUSTMENT button to adjust the time as you like. The TIME ADJUSTMENT button allows you to customize the amount of time your food is going to spend cooking. You may use this button to set your preferred time.

  However, it appears that you may only be able to increase the cooking time using the TIME ADJUSTMENT button, you may not be able to reduce the time (minutes) using this button. If you need to reduce the minutes your food is going to spend cooking after you have set a higher time, press the KEEP WARM/CANCEL button and then press a food button corresponding to the time you want to cook. If you need to increase the cook time, press the TIME ADJUSTMENT button.
- You can use the COOK TIME SELECTOR button to adjust the default time for a specific food program. For example, when you press the SLOW COOK button, the default time is 2 hours, but you can use the COOK TIME SELECTOR button to adjust it to 6 hours or 12 hours. Also you can use

COOK TIME SELECTOR button to select the preferred program for White, Brown or Wild rice.
- You don't need to follow the 30-day recipes sequentially. There is nothing wrong if you cook the recipe for Day 15 after cooking the recipe for day 1.
- Please feel free to change the ingredients mentioned in the recipes if you think you know of better ingredients.

Day 1 – Spinach and Mushroom Frittata

Servings: 6 to 8

Ingredients:

- 1 teaspoon coconut oil
- 1 small yellow onion, chopped
- 10 ounces sliced mushrooms
- 2 cups chopped spinach
- 8 large eggs, whisked well
- 2 tablespoons water
- Salt and pepper to taste

Instructions:

1. Add the coconut oil to the inner pot of your Power Pressure Cooker XL.
2. Pour in the onions and mushrooms.

3. Cook the vegetables on the Sauté setting until they are tender. You can use the CHICKEN/MEAT button to sauté (there is no browning or sauté button).
4. Add the spinach and cook for 1 minute or until just wilted.
5. Spread the vegetables evenly in the bottom of the cooker.
6. In a mixing bowl, whisk the eggs with the water, salt and pepper.
7. Pour the eggs into the pressure cooker then close the lid and the pressure valve.
8. Bring the cooker to high pressure by pressing the FISH/VEGETABLES/STEAM button. Allow to cook for 1 minute and press KEEP WARM/CANCEL.
9. Allow the cooker to naturally depressurize for 5-10 minutes and then carefully release the remaining pressure manually and then let the frittata cool for a few minutes before serving.

Note: You don't need to close the pressure cooker with the pressure lid while sautéing your food. If you must close the pressure cooker, then don't close the pressure valve or you may just close the pressure cooker with a glass lid (if you have one).

Day 2 – Honey Cinnamon Steel-Cut Oats

Servings: 4 to 6

Ingredients:

- 1 tablespoon coconut oil
- 1 ½ cups steel-cut oats
- 3 ½ cups water
- 4 to 6 tablespoons honey
- 1 ½ teaspoon ground cinnamon
- Pinch of salt

Instructions:

1. Melt the coconut oil in your Power Pressure Cooker XL on the Sauté setting. You can use the CHICKEN/MEAT button to sauté (there is no browning or sauté button).
2. Stir in the steel-cut oats and sauté for 2 to 3 minutes until toasted.

3. Add the water, honey, cinnamon and salt.
4. Close the lid and the pressure valve then bring the cooker to high pressure (you can press the SOUP/STEW button) and cook for 10 minutes.
5. After the timer reaches 0, the cooker will automatically enter **KEEP WARM** mode. Press the CANCEL button and allow the cooker to naturally depressurize for 5-10 minutes. Then carefully release the remaining pressure manually and open the lid.
6. Stir the oats well then close the lid and let them thicken for 10 minutes before serving.

Day 3 – Sausage and Egg Casserole

Servings: 6 to 8

Ingredients:
- 1 teaspoon coconut oil

- ½ pound ground chicken sausage
- 1 small red pepper, cored and chopped
- 1 cup fresh chopped spinach
- 1 small red onion, chopped
- 1 medium tomato, sliced thin
- 8 large eggs, whisked
- 2 tablespoons water
- Salt and pepper to taste

Instructions:
1. Add the coconut oil to the inner pot of your Power Pressure Cooker XL.
2. Place the sausage in the cooker and cook on the Sauté setting until browned. You can use the CHICKEN/MEAT button to brown (there is no browning or sauté button).
3. Drain the extra grease from the cooker then stir in the red pepper, spinach, and onions.
4. Cook the vegetables on the Sauté setting until they are tender. You can use the CHICKEN/MEAT button to sauté (there is no browning or sauté button).
5. Spread the vegetables evenly then top the mixture with slices of tomato.
6. In a mixing bowl, whisk the eggs with the water, salt and pepper.
7. Pour the eggs into the pressure cooker then close the lid and the pressure valve.

8. Bring the cooker to high pressure by pressing the FISH/VEGETABLES/STEAM button. Allow to cook for 1 minute and press KEEP WARM/CANCEL.
9. Allow the cooker to naturally depressurize for 5-10 minutes and then carefully release the remaining pressure manually. Let the casserole cool for a few minutes before serving.

Day 4 – Sweet Raspberry Jam

Servings: makes 3 pints

Ingredients:

- 9 to 10 cups fresh raspberries
- ¼ cup pectin powder
- 6 cups evaporated cane sugar

Instructions:

1. Pour the raspberries into the inner pot of your Power Pressure Cooker XL then sprinkle in the pectin.
2. Stir in the sugar until it is all well combined.
3. Turn on the pressure cooker to the Sauté setting then wait for it to boil. You can use the CHICKEN/MEAT button to sauté (there is no browning or sauté button).
4. Cook the mixture for 2 minutes or so then turn off the cooker.

5. Spoon the jam mixture into 3 clean pint jars and cover each with a lid.
6. Place the jars in your pressure cooker and pack clean towels around them so they don't rattle against each other.
7. Pour in enough water to cover the jars then close the lid but leave the pressure valve open.
8. Leaving the pressure valve opened, turn the pressure cooker on to high heat (you may press the MEAT/CHICKEN button to achieve the high heat) and wait for the water to boil.
9. Then cook the jam for another 2-5 minutes.
10. Press the CANCEL/KEEP WARM button and take the jars out of the cooker to cool.

Day 5 – Creamy Maple Apple Oatmeal

Servings: 4 to 6

Ingredients:

- 1 tablespoon coconut oil
- 1 ½ cups steel-cut oats
- 3 cups water
- ½ cup unsweetened applesauce
- 4 tablespoons maple syrup
- 1 ½ teaspoon ground cinnamon
- Pinch of salt

Instructions:

1. Melt the coconut oil in your Power Pressure Cooker XL on the Sauté setting. You can use the CHICKEN/MEAT button to sauté (there is no browning or sauté button).

2. Stir in the steel-cut oats and sauté for 2 to 3 minutes until toasted.
3. Add the water, maple syrup, applesauce, cinnamon and salt.
4. Close the lid and the pressure valve then bring the cooker to high pressure (you can press the SOUP/STEW button) and cook for 10 minutes.
5. After the timer reaches 0, the cooker will automatically enter **KEEP WARM** mode. Press the CANCEL button and allow the cooker to naturally depressurize for 5-10 minutes. Then carefully release the remaining pressure manually and open the lid.
6. Stir the oats well then close the lid and let them thicken for 10 minutes.
7. Spoon the oatmeal into bowls and serve with raisins or other dried fruit.

Day 6 – Chocolate Berry Breakfast Cake

Servings: 6 to 8

Ingredients:

- 5 large eggs, whisked
- ¼ cup white sugar
- 2 tablespoons melted coconut oil
- ¾ cups part-skim ricotta cheese
- ¾ cups plain non-fat yogurt
- 1 teaspoon vanilla extract
- 1 cup pastry flour
- ½ tablespoon baking powder
- ½ teaspoon salt
- 1 cup fresh berries (your choice)
- Chocolate syrup, to serve

Instructions:

1. Grease a Bundt cake pan with cooking spray and make sure it fits in the Power Pressure Cooker XL.
2. In a mixing bowl, beat together the eggs and sugar.
3. Beat in the coconut oil, ricotta cheese, yogurt and vanilla until smooth and combined.
4. In another bowl, whisk together your flour, baking powder and salt.
5. Stir together the wet and dry ingredients then pour it into the prepared pan.
6. Sprinkle the berries into the wet batter.
7. Place a steamer tray in the pressure cooker and add 1 cup water. Make sure the steamer tray sits properly. The steamer tray is hollow tray that came with your Power Pressure Cooker XL. Please note that you can also use a wire rack instead of steamer tray.
8. Then place the Bundt cake pan on the steamer tray in the cooker and close the lid.
9. Close the lid and the pressure valve then bring the cooker to high pressure and cook for 25 minutes. To get 25 minutes cook time, you can press the Rice/Risotto button and then use the cook time selector to adjust to 25 minutes.
10. After the timer reaches 0, the cooker will automatically enter **KEEP WARM** mode. Press the CANCEL button and allow the cooker to naturally depressurize for 5-10 minutes. Then carefully release the remaining pressure manually and open the lid.

11. Remove the pan and let the cake cool for 10 minutes before turning it out onto a plate.
12. Drizzle with chocolate syrup and slice to serve.

Day 7 – Tomato Basil Frittata

Servings: 6 to 8

Ingredients:

- 1 teaspoon coconut oil
- 2 medium tomatoes, cored and chopped
- 1 small red pepper, cored and chopped
- ½ red onion, chopped
- ¼ cup fresh chopped basil
- 8 large eggs, whisked well
- 2 tablespoons water
- Salt and pepper to taste

Instructions:

1. Add the coconut oil to the inner pot of your Power Pressure Cooker XL.
2. Pour in the tomatoes, red peppers, and onions.

3. Cook the vegetables on the Sauté setting until they are tender. You can use the CHICKEN/MEAT button to sauté (there is no browning or sauté button).
4. Spread the vegetables evenly then sprinkle with fresh chopped basil.
5. In a mixing bowl, whisk the eggs with the water, salt and pepper.
6. Pour the eggs into the inner pot of your pressure cooker then close the lid and the pressure valve.
7. Bring the cooker to high pressure by pressing the FISH/VEGETABLES/STEAM button. Allow to cook for 1 minute and press KEEP WARM/CANCEL.
8. Allow the cooker to naturally depressurize for 5-10 minutes and then carefully release the remaining pressure manually. Let the frittata cool for a few minutes before serving.

Day 8 – Cinnamon Baked French Toast

Servings: 6 to 8

Ingredients:

- ¼ cup coconut oil, melted
- ½ cup coconut sugar
- 2 cups unsweetened coconut milk
- 3 large eggs, whisked
- 1 teaspoon vanilla extract
- 1 teaspoon ground cinnamon
- Pinch of salt
- 1 loaf fresh Italian bread, cut into cubes

Instructions:

1. Whisk together the melted coconut oil and coconut sugar in a large mixing bowl.

2. Add in the coconut milk, eggs, vanilla extract, cinnamon and salt.
3. Toss in the cubed bread until it soaks up the mixture in the bowl.
4. Liberally grease a cake pan with extra coconut oil – make sure it fits in your pressure cooker.
5. Pour the bread mixture into the cake pan.
6. Add a steamer tray to your Power Pressure Cooker XL and pour in 1 cup of water. The steamer tray is hollow tray that came with your Power Pressure Cooker XL. Please note that you can also use a wire rack instead of steamer tray.
7. Place the cake pan on top of the steamer tray.
8. Close the lid and the pressure valve then bring the cooker to high pressure and cook for 25 minutes. To get 25 minutes cook time, you can press the Rice/Risotto button and then use the cook time selector to adjust to 25 minutes.
9. After the timer reaches 0, the cooker will automatically enter **KEEP WARM** mode. Press the CANCEL button, carefully release the pressure and then open the lid.
10. Take the cake pan out of the pressure cooker then cut the French toast and serve hot.

Day 9 – Hearty Beef and Red Bean Chili

Servings: 6 to 8

Ingredients:

- 1 teaspoon coconut oil
- 2 pounds lean ground beef
- Salt and pepper to taste
- 1 ¼ cups beef broth (low-sodium)
- ¼ cup tomato paste
- 1 large yellow onion, chopped
- 2 ½ tablespoons chili powder
- 1 tablespoon ground cumin
- 3 cloves minced garlic
- 2 (15-ounce) cans red kidney beans, rinsed and drained
- 2 (15-ounce) cans diced tomatoes

Instructions:
1. Melt the coconut oil in your Power Pressure Cooker XL on the Sauté setting. You can use the CHICKEN/MEAT button to sauté (there is no browning or sauté button).
2. Add the ground beef and some salt and pepper.
3. Cook the beef until it is browned then drains the grease from the cooker.
4. In a bowl, stir together the beef broth and tomato paste.
5. Pour the onions into the cooker along with the beef broth mixture, the chili powder, cumin, and garlic.
6. Add the beans and tomatoes then stir everything together.
7. Close the lid and the pressure valve then bring the cooker to high pressure (you can press the SOUP/STEW button) and cook for 10 minutes.
8. After the timer reaches 0, the cooker will automatically enter **KEEP WARM** mode. Press the CANCEL button and allow the cooker to naturally depressurize for 5-10 minutes. Then carefully release the remaining pressure manually and open the lid.
9. Adjust the seasoning to taste and serve hot.

Day 10 – Split Pea and Smoked Turkey Soup

Servings: 6 to 8

Ingredients:

- 1 tablespoon coconut oil
- 1 large sweet onion, chopped
- 2 large stalks celery, diced
- 2 cloves minced garlic
- 1 pound dried split peas, rinsed and drained
- 6 cups low-sodium vegetable broth
- Salt and pepper to taste
- 2 smoked turkey thighs or drumsticks

Instructions:

1. Melt the coconut oil in your Power Pressure Cooker XL on the Sauté setting. You can use the CHICKEN/MEAT button to sauté (there is no browning or sauté button).
2. Add the onions, celery, and garlic then cook for 3 to 4 minutes until the onions start to soften.
3. Pour in the split peas along with the rest of the ingredients, including the smoked turkey thigh or drumsticks.
4. Close the lid and the pressure valve then bring the cooker to high pressure (you can press the SOUP/STEW button) and cook for 10 minutes.

5. After the timer reaches 0, the cooker will automatically enter **KEEP WARM** mode. Press the CANCEL button and allow the cooker to naturally depressurize for 5-10 minutes. Then carefully release the remaining pressure manually and open the lid.
6. Remove the smoked turkey thigh and chop the meat off the bone – set it aside.
7. Use an immersion blender to puree the soup or do it in batches using your blender.
8. Spoon the soup into bowls and serve topped with diced turkey thigh or drumsticks.

Day 11 – Beef and Vegetable Stew

Servings: 6 to 8

Ingredients:

- 1 tablespoon coconut oil
- 3 pounds beef stew meat, chopped
- Salt and pepper to taste
- 8 ounces sliced white mushrooms
- 2 cups beef broth (low-sodium)
- ¼ cup tomato paste
- 2 tablespoons Soy sauce (please omit this ingredient if you are allergic to soy products)
- 2 medium yellow onions, chopped
- 3 large carrots, sliced
- 2 stalks celery, sliced
- 3 cloves minced garlic

- 2 cups chopped potatoes

Instructions:
1. Melt the coconut oil in your Power Pressure Cooker XL on the Sauté setting. You can use the CHICKEN/MEAT button to sauté (there is no browning or sauté button).
2. Season the beef with salt and pepper then add it to the cooker.
3. Sauté the beef until it is evenly browned then spoon it off into a bowl. You can use the CHICKEN/MEAT button to sauté (there is no browning or sauté button).
4. Pour the mushrooms into the cooker and let them cook.
5. Meanwhile, whisk together the beef broth, tomato paste, and soy sauce.
6. Add the onions, carrots, celery, and garlic to the cooker.
7. Cook the vegetables and mushrooms until tender.
8. Pour the broth mixture into the cooker and add the potatoes and seasonings.
9. Close the lid and the pressure valve and then cook the soup for 4 minutes. To get 4-minutes cook time, press FISH/VEGETABLES/STEAM button and use the COOK TIME SELECTOR button to adjust the cook time to 4 minutes.
10. After the timer reaches 0, the cooker will automatically enter **KEEP WARM** mode. Press the CANCEL button and allow the cooker to naturally depressurize for 5-10 minutes. Then carefully release the remaining pressure manually.

11. Lift the lid then spoon half of the vegetable mixture into a bowl and set aside.
12. Add the beef to the cooker then close the lid and the pressure valve.
13. Let the stew cook for 30 minutes. To get 30-minutes cook time, press the SOUP/STEW button and use the COOK TIME SELECTOR button to adjust the cook time to 30 minutes.
14. After the timer reaches 0, the cooker will automatically enter **KEEP WARM** mode. Press the CANCEL button and allow the cooker to naturally depressurize for 5-10 minutes. Then carefully release the remaining pressure manually and open the lid.
15. Stir the reserved vegetables back into the cooker then spoon the stew into bowls and serve hot.

Note: If you are allergic to soy products, please omit the soy sauce in the recipe above.

Day 12 – New England Clam Chowder

Servings: 6 to 8

Ingredients:

- 3 (14-ounce) cans minced clams
- 1 teaspoon coconut oil
- ½ pound thick turkey bacon, chopped
- 1 medium yellow onion, chopped
- 1 clove minced garlic
- 3 cups Yukon gold potatoes, chopped
- 1 (15-ounce) can full-fat coconut milk
- 2 cups unsweetened coconut milk beverage
- Salt and pepper to taste

Instructions:
1. Drain the canned clams, pouring the liquid into a bowl.
2. Add enough water to the clam liquid to make about 4 cups.

3. Melt the coconut oil in your Power Pressure Cooker XL on the Sauté setting. You can use the CHICKEN/MEAT button to sauté (there is no browning or sauté button).
4. Add the chopped bacon and Sauté until it is browned then remove to a bowl using a slotted spoon. You can use the CHICKEN/MEAT button to sauté (there is no browning or sauté button).
5. Pour in the onions and garlic then cook for 3 to 4 minutes until the onions start to soften.
6. Add the potatoes along with the clam liquid and the salt and pepper.
7. Cover the pressure cooker with the lid and close the pressure valve.
8. Cook the soup for 10 minutes. To get 10-minutes cook time, press the SOUP/STEW button.
9. After the timer reaches 0, the cooker will automatically enter **KEEP WARM** mode. Press the CANCEL button and allow the cooker to naturally depressurize for 5-10 minutes. Then carefully release the remaining pressure manually.
10. Lift the lid and disconnect the pressure cooker from the power source.
11. Stir the canned coconut milk and unsweetened coconut milk along with the clams.
12. Spoon the soup into bowls and serve hot.

Day 13 – Herbed Butternut Squash Soup

Servings: 6 to 8

Ingredients:

- 1 tablespoon coconut oil
- 1 large yellow onion, chopped
- 3 cloves minced garlic
- 4 cups butternut squash cubes
- 3 cups low-sodium vegetable broth
- 1 teaspoon dried rosemary
- ½ teaspoon dried thyme
- ½ teaspoon dried sage
- Salt and pepper to taste

Instructions:

1. Melt the coconut oil in your Power Pressure Cooker XL on the Sauté setting. You can use the CHICKEN/MEAT button to sauté (there is no browning or sauté button).
2. Add the onions and garlic then cook for 3 to 4 minutes until the onions start to soften.
3. Pour in the butternut squash cubes along with the rest of the ingredients.
4. Cover the pressure cooker with the lid and close the pressure valve.
5. Cook the soup for 10 minutes. To get 10-minutes cook time, press the SOUP/STEW button.
6. After the timer reaches 0, the cooker will automatically enter **KEEP WARM** mode. Press the CANCEL button and allow the cooker to naturally depressurize for 5-10 minutes. Then carefully release the remaining pressure manually.
7. Lift the lid and disconnect the pressure cooker from the power source.
8. Use an immersion blender to puree the soup or do it in batches using your blender.
9. Spoon the soup into bowls and serve hot.

Day 14 – Lentil and Carrot Soup

Servings: 6 to 8

Ingredients:

- 1 teaspoon coconut oil
- 1 medium yellow onion, chopped
- 2 large carrots, chopped
- 2 stalks celery chopped
- 3 cloves minced garlic
- 4 cups low-sodium vegetable broth
- 1 cup uncooked red lentils, rinsed and drained
- 1 teaspoon ground cumin
- 2 small bay leaves
- Salt and pepper to taste

Instructions:

1. Melt the coconut oil in your Power Pressure Cooker XL on the Sauté setting. You can use the CHICKEN/MEAT button to sauté (there is no browning or sauté button).
2. Add the onions, carrots, celery and garlic then cook for 3 to 4 minutes until the onions start to soften.
3. Pour in the vegetable broth, lentils, cumin and bay leaf.
4. Cover the pressure cooker with the lid and close the pressure valve.
5. Let the soup cook for 20 minutes. To get 20-minutes cook time, press the SOUP/STEW button and use the TIME ADJUSTMENT button to adjust the cook time to 20 minutes.
6. After the timer reaches 0, the cooker will automatically enter **KEEP WARM** mode. Press the CANCEL button and carefully release the pressure.
7. Lift the lid and disconnect the pressure cooker from the power source – remove the bay leaf.
8. Adjust seasoning to taste and spoon the soup into bowls and serve hot.

Day 15 – Squash, Spinach and White Bean Soup

Servings: 6 to 8

Ingredients:

- 2 teaspoons coconut oil
- 1 large sweet onion, chopped
- 3 large stalks celery, sliced
- 3 cloves minced garlic
- 1 pound dried white beans, rinsed and drained
- 8 cups low-sodium chicken broth
- 1 teaspoon fresh chopped thyme
- 1 teaspoon fresh chopped rosemary
- Salt and pepper to taste
- 3 cups fresh cubed butternut squash
- 4 cups chopped spinach

Instructions:

1. Melt the coconut oil in your Power Pressure Cooker XL on the Sauté setting. You can use the CHICKEN/MEAT button to sauté (there is no browning or sauté button).
2. Add the onions, celery and garlic then cook for 3 to 4 minutes until the onions start to soften.
3. Pour in the white beans and chicken broth along with the herbs and seasonings.
4. Cover the pressure cooker with the lid and close the pressure valve.
5. Let the soup cook for 15 minutes. To get 15-minutes cook time, press the SOUP/STEW button and use the TIME ADJUSTMENT button to adjust the cook time to 15 minutes.
6. After the timer reaches 0, the cooker will automatically enter **KEEP WARM** mode. Press the CANCEL button and allow the cooker to naturally depressurize for 5-10 minutes. Then carefully release the remaining pressure manually.
7. Lift the lid and add the butternut squash.
8. Cover the pressure cooker with the lid and close the pressure valve.
9. Cook the soup for another 10 minutes. To get 10-minutes cook time, press the SOUP/STEW button.
10. After the timer reaches 0, the cooker will automatically enter **KEEP WARM** mode. Press the CANCEL button, carefully release the pressure and then open the lid.
11. Stir in the chopped spinach then spoon the soup into bowls and serve hot.

Day 16 – Beef and Mushroom Stroganoff

Servings: 6 to 8

Ingredients:

- 1 tablespoon coconut oil
- 2 ½ pounds boneless beef sirloin, cubed
- Salt and pepper to taste
- 2 cups water
- 1 large yellow onion, chopped
- 2 (10.5) cans cream of mushroom soup
- 2 (10.5) cans condensed mushroom soup
- 12 ounces light sour cream
- 1 cup canned coconut milk
- Fresh egg noodles, to serve

Note: some mushroom soups may contain soy products which may be inappropriate for someone allergic to soybean, remember to check the ingredients before buying them.

Instructions:
1. Melt the oil in your Power Pressure Cooker XL on the Sauté setting. You can use the CHICKEN/MEAT button to sauté (there is no browning or sauté button).
2. Season the beef with salt and pepper then add it to the cooker along with the water and onion.
3. Cook for 3 minutes until the onions start to soften.
4. Close the lid and pressure valve. Cook for 20 minutes. To get 20-minutes cook time, press the SOUP/STEW button and use the TIME ADJUSTMENT button to adjust the cook time to 20 minutes.
5. After the timer reaches 0, the cooker will automatically enter **KEEP WARM** mode. Press the CANCEL button and allow the cooker to naturally depressurize for 5-10 minutes. Then carefully release the remaining pressure manually and open the lid.
6. Drain all but ¾ cup of the cooking liquid then stir in the remaining ingredients.
7. Simmer the mixture on the Sauté setting until the sauce thickens. You can use the CHICKEN/MEAT button to sauté (there is no browning or sauté button).
8. Serve the stroganoff hot over fresh egg noodles.

Day 17 – Braised Lamb Shanks

Servings: 6 to 8

Ingredients:

- 2 tablespoons coconut oil, divided
- 3 medium tomatoes
- 8 bone-in lamb shanks, trimmed
- ¼ cup flour
- 1 large onion, chopped
- 2 large carrots, peeled and sliced
- 2 cloves minced garlic
- 1 cup cranberry juice
- ½ cup beef stock (low-sodium)
- 1 tablespoon fresh chopped oregano
- 2 teaspoons lemon zest
- Salt and pepper to taste

Instructions:
1. Bring a pot of water to boil then add the tomatoes and boil for 1 minute.
2. Remove the tomatoes to an ice bath them peel them and cut into quarters.
3. Heat 1 tablespoon of coconut oil in your Power Pressure Cooker XL on the Sauté setting. You can use the CHICKEN/MEAT button to sauté (there is no browning or sauté button).
4. Toss the lamb shanks in flour then add to the cooker.
5. Cook the lamb shanks until they are browned then remove to a bowl.
6. Heat the remaining oil in the cooker then add the carrots, onion, and garlic.
7. Cook for 5 minutes then stir in the tomatoes, cranberry juice, beef stock, and seasonings.
8. Bring the mixture to boil then add the lamb shanks.
9. Close the lid and the pressure valve then bring the cooker to high pressure and cook for 25 minutes. To get 25 minutes cook time, you can press the SOUP/STEW button and then use the TIME ADJUSTMENT button to adjust to 25 minutes.
10. After the timer reaches 0, the cooker will automatically enter **KEEP WARM** mode. Press the CANCEL button and allow the cooker to naturally depressurize for 5-10 minutes. Then carefully release the remaining pressure manually and open the lid.

11. To thicken the gravy, cook the sauce uncovered on the Sauté setting for a few minutes.
12. Serve and enjoy!

Day 18 – Raspberry Glazed Chicken

Servings: 6 to 8

Ingredients:

- ¾ cups cranberry juice
- 1 ¼ cup raspberry jam
- ¼ cup honey
- 1 tablespoon Dijon mustard
- 3 cloves minced garlic
- 5 to 6 pounds whole chicken legs

Instructions:

1. Whisk together the cranberry juice, jam, honey, mustard and garlic in a small bowl.
2. Place the chicken in the inner pot of your Power Pressure Cooker XL.

3. Pour in the marinade then cover and chill in the fridge overnight.
4. Place the insert back in the pressure cooker and bring it to a boil on the Sauté setting. You can use the CHICKEN/MEAT button to sauté (there is no browning or sauté button).
13. Close the lid and the pressure valve then cook for 12 minutes. To get 12-minutes cook time, press the SOUP/STEW button and then use the TIME ADJUSTMENT button to adjust to 12 minutes.
5. After the timer reaches 0, the cooker will automatically enter **KEEP WARM** mode. Press the CANCEL button and allow the cooker to naturally depressurize for 5-10 minutes. Then carefully release the remaining pressure manually and open the lid.
6. Let the chicken cook on the Sauté setting until the sauce thickens then serve hot.

Day 19 – Creamy Mushroom Risotto

Servings: 6 to 8

Ingredients:

- 6 tablespoons coconut oil
- 1 large yellow onion, chopped
- 3 cloves minced garlic
- 12 ounces sliced portabella mushrooms
- 2 cups Arborio rice
- 5 cups low-sodium chicken broth
- 1 ½ cups grated parmesan cheese

Instructions:

1. Melt the oil in your Power Pressure Cooker XL on the Sauté setting. You can use the CHICKEN/MEAT button to sauté (there is no browning or sauté button).

2. Add the onions and garlic and cook for 3 minutes until they start to soften.
3. Stir in the mushrooms and rice until coated with oil then pour in the chicken broth.
4. Close the lid and the pressure valve then cook for 7 minutes. To get 7-minutes cook time, press the SOUP/STEW button and then use the TIME ADJUSTMENT button to adjust to 7 minutes.
5. After the timer reaches 0, the cooker will automatically enter **KEEP WARM** mode. Press the CANCEL button and allow the cooker to naturally depressurize for 5-10 minutes. Then carefully release the remaining pressure manually and open the lid.
6. Stir in the parmesan cheese and serve hot.

Day 20 – Easy Chicken Cacciatore

Servings: 6 to 8

Ingredients:

- 1 tablespoon coconut oil
- 1 large yellow onion, chopped
- 2 medium red peppers, cored and chopped
- ¾ cups of ginger ale
- 16 ounces sliced mushrooms
- 4 cloves minced garlic
- 4 pounds bone-in skinless chicken thighs
- 2 (14-ounce) cans crushed tomatoes
- 3 tablespoons tomato paste
- 1 cup sliced black olives
- ¼ cup fresh chopped parsley
- Salt and pepper to taste

Instructions:

1. Melt the oil in your Power Pressure Cooker XL on the Sauté setting. You can use the CHICKEN/MEAT button to sauté (there is no browning or sauté button).
2. Add the onions and peppers and cook for 3 minutes until they start to soften.
3. Stir in the ginger ale and let it cook until it boils then scrape up any browned bits.
4. Add the mushrooms and garlic then place the chicken on top.
5. Pour the crushed tomatoes over the chicken and add the tomato paste on top.
6. Close the lid and the pressure valve then cook for 8 minutes. To get 8-minutes cook time, press the Fish/Veg./Steam button and then use the TIME ADJUSTMENT button to adjust to 8 minutes.
7. After the timer reaches 0, the cooker will automatically enter **KEEP WARM** mode. Press the CANCEL button and allow the cooker to naturally depressurize for 5-10 minutes. Then carefully release the remaining pressure manually and open the lid.
8. Stir in the olives and seasonings then serve hot.

Day 21 – Beef Burgundy with Egg Noodles

Servings: 6 to 8

Ingredients:

- 1 tablespoon coconut oil
- 1 ¼ pounds boneless beef stew meat, chopped
- Salt and pepper to taste
- 16 ounces sliced mushrooms
- 12 ounces white pearl onions, peeled
- 1 ¾ cups unsweetened cranberry juice
- 2 teaspoons dried thyme
- ¼ cup flour
- ¼ cup water
- Fresh egg noodles, to serve

Instructions:

1. Melt the oil in your Power Pressure Cooker XL on the Sauté setting. You can use the CHICKEN/MEAT button to sauté (there is no browning or sauté button).
2. Season the beef with salt and pepper then add it to the cooker.
3. Cook the beef until browned then remove it to a plate.
4. Add the mushrooms and onions to the cooker and cook for 3 minutes until they start to soften.
5. Pour in the unsweetened cranberry juice and scrape up any browned bits.
6. Add the beef back to the cooker along with the thyme then close the lid.
7. Close the lid and the pressure valve then cook for 15 minutes. To get 15-minutes cook time, press the MEAT/CHICKEN button.
8. After the timer reaches 0, the cooker will automatically enter **KEEP WARM** mode. Press the CANCEL button and allow the cooker to naturally depressurize for 5-10 minutes. Then carefully release the remaining pressure manually and open the lid.
9. Whisk the flour and water together then stir into the cooker.
10. Cook on the Sauté setting until the sauce thickens then serve hot over fresh egg noodles.

Day 22 – Vegan Chickpea Curry

Servings: 6 to 8

Ingredients:

- 1 tablespoon coconut oil
- 1 large yellow onion, sliced
- 4 cloves minced garlic
- 2 teaspoons ground coriander
- 2 teaspoons ground cumin
- 2 teaspoons garam masala
- 2 teaspoons ground turmeric
- 2 (15-ounce) cans chickpeas, rinsed and drained
- 2 (14-ounce) cans diced tomatoes
- 4 medium Yukon gold potatoes, chopped
- ¼ cup fresh chopped parsley
- Salt and pepper to taste

Instructions:

1. Melt the oil in your Power Pressure Cooker XL on the Sauté setting. You can use the CHICKEN/MEAT button to sauté (there is no browning or sauté button).
2. Add the onions and cook for 3 minutes until they start to soften.
3. Stir in the garlic, coriander, cumin, garam masala and turmeric and cook for 1 minute.
4. Pour in the rest of the ingredients then close the lid and the pressure valve.
5. Cook for 15 minutes. To get 15-minutes cook time, press the Fish/Veg./Steam button and then use the TIME ADJUSTMENT button to adjust to 15 minutes.
6. After the timer reaches 0, the cooker will automatically enter **KEEP WARM** mode. Press the CANCEL button and allow the cooker to naturally depressurize for 5-10 minutes. Then carefully release the remaining pressure manually and open the lid.
7. Stir in the fresh parsley and season with salt and pepper.
8. Serve the curry hot over steamed rice.

Day 23 – Corned Beef and Cabbage

Servings: 6 to 8

Ingredients:

- 1 (2 ½ to 3 pound) corned beef brisket
- 3 cloves minced garlic
- 2 small bay leaves
- 1 large head cabbage, cut into wedges
- 6 medium Yukon gold potatoes, quartered
- 6 carrots, cut into chunks
- 4 cups of water

Instructions:

1. Pour 4 cups of water into your Power Pressure Cooker XL.

2. Place the brisket in the cooker then turn it to the high heat setting (you may press the CHICKEN/MEAT button to achieve high heat) and wait for the water to boil.
3. Skim off the foam then sprinkle in the garlic and bay leaf – close the lid and the pressure valve.
4. Cook for 1 hour 15 minutes. To get 1 hour 15-minutes cook time, press the Meat/Chicken button and then use the TIME ADJUSTMENT button to adjust to 1 hour 15 minutes.
5. After the timer reaches 0, the cooker will automatically enter **KEEP WARM** mode. Press the CANCEL button and allow the cooker to naturally depressurize for 5-10 minutes. Then carefully release the remaining pressure manually and open the lid.
6. Add the cabbage, potatoes and carrots to the cooker then stir well.
7. Close the lid and the pressure valve again and then cook for 6 minutes. To get 6-minutes cook time, press the Fish/Veg./Steam button and then use the TIME ADJUSTMENT button to adjust to 6 minutes.
8. After the timer reaches 0, the cooker will automatically enter **KEEP WARM** mode. Press the CANCEL button and allow the cooker to naturally depressurize for 5-10 minutes. Then carefully release the remaining pressure manually and open the lid.
9. Serve and enjoy!

Day 24 – Chocolate Coconut Rice Pudding

Servings: 6 to 8

Ingredients:

- 1 ½ cups water
- 1 cup uncooked Arborio rice
- Pinch of salt
- 2 cups unsweetened coconut milk
- ½ cup coconut sugar
- 2 large eggs, whisked
- 3 tablespoons unsweetened cocoa powder
- 1 teaspoon vanilla extract
- ½ cup unsweetened shredded coconut

Instructions:

1. Combine the water, Arborio rice, and salt in your Power Pressure Cooker XL.

10. Close the lid and bring the cooker to high pressure – cook for 3 minutes. To get 3-minutes cook time, press the Fish/Veg./Steam button and then use the TIME ADJUSTMENT button to adjust to 3 minutes.
2. After the timer reaches 0, the cooker will automatically enter **KEEP WARM** mode. Press the CANCEL button and allow the cooker to naturally depressurize for 10 minutes. Then carefully release the remaining pressure manually and open the lid.
3. Stir in 1 ½ cups of coconut milk along with the coconut sugar.
4. In a small mixing bowl, whisk together the eggs, cocoa powder and vanilla extract with the rest of the coconut milk.
5. Strain the liquid through cheesecloth and stir it into the mixture in the pressure cooker.
6. Turn the pressure cooker on the sauté setting and cook, stirring often, until the mixture comes to a boil.
7. Turn off the heat by pressing CANCEL/KEEP WARM button and stir in the shredded coconut then let the pudding cool before serving.

Day 25 – Easy Baked Apples

Servings: 8

Ingredients:

- 8 small ripe apples
- 1 ¼ cups of water
- ½ cup seedless raisins
- ¼ cup finely chopped walnuts
- ¼ cup brown sugar
- 1 teaspoon ground cinnamon

Instructions:

1. Use a sharp knife to cut the core out of each apple from the top.
2. Place the apples in your Power Pressure Cooker XL.
3. Pour the water into the pressure cooker around the apples.

4. Combine the raisins, walnuts, brown sugar and cinnamon in a bowl.
5. Spoon the raisin mixture into the cored apples then close the lid and the pressure valve.
6. Cook for 10 minutes. To get 10-minutes cook time, press the SOUP/STEW button.
7. After the timer reaches 0, the cooker will automatically enter **KEEP WARM** mode. Press the CANCEL button and allow the cooker to naturally depressurize for 5-10 minutes. Then carefully release the remaining pressure manually and open the lid.
8. Scoop out the apples into individual bowls and serve them warm.

Day 26 – Chocolate Cookie Cheesecake

Servings: 10 to 12

Ingredients:

- 20 chocolate cookies
- 2/3 cups plus 1 tablespoon sugar
- ¼ cup melted coconut oil
- 2 tablespoons cornstarch
- Pinch of salt
- 2 (8-ounce) packages reduced fat cream cheese
- ½ cup light sour cream
- 1 teaspoon vanilla extract

Instructions:

1. Reserve six of the chocolate cookies then place the rest in a food processor.

2. Pulse the cookies until they are finely ground then stir in 1 tablespoon of sugar.
3. Pour the mixture into a small bowl then stir in the melted coconut oil.
4. Line a cheesecake pan with parchment then press the cookie mixture into the bottom to form the crust.
5. Bake the crust at 325°F for 15 minutes then set aside to cool.
6. Combine the rest of the sugar in a mixing bowl with the cornstarch and salt.
7. In another bowl, beat together the cream cheese and sugar mixture until it is thick and creamy.
8. Add the sour cream and vanilla extract then beat until combined.
9. Beat in the eggs one at a time then break the reserved cookies into pieces and fold them in.
10. Pour the mixture into the cheesecake pan.
11. Place a steamer tray in your Power Pressure Cooker XL then pour in 1 cup of water.
12. Put the cheesecake pan on top of the steamer tray then close the lid and the pressure valve.
13. Cook the cheesecake for 26 minutes. To get 26-minutes cook time, press the Fish/Veg./Steam button and then use the TIME ADJUSTMENT button to adjust to 26 minutes.
14. After the timer reaches 0, the cooker will automatically enter **KEEP WARM** mode. Press the CANCEL button and allow the cooker to naturally depressurize for 5-10 minutes. Then

carefully release the remaining pressure manually and open the lid.
15. Remove the cheesecake and let it cool to room temperature.
16. Chill the cheesecake for several hours before serving.

Day 27 – Vanilla Poached Pears

Servings: 6

Ingredients:

- 3 cups water
- 2 cups dry ginger ale
- 2 cups white sugar
- 2 vanilla beans, split and seeds scraped out
- 6 medium-sized ripe pears
- Fresh berries

Instructions:

1. Combine the water, ginger ale, sugar, and vanilla beans in your Power Pressure Cooker XL.
2. Turn the cooker on to the Sauté setting and let it heat up while you peel the pears. You can use the CHICKEN/MEAT button to sauté (there is no browning or sauté button).

3. Stir in the lemon juice then cut the pears in half down the middle and add them to the cooker.
4. Close the lid and the pressure valve – cook the pears for 3 minutes. To get 3-minutes cook time, press the Fish/Veg./Steam button and then use the TIME ADJUSTMENT button to adjust to 3 minutes.
5. After the timer reaches 0, the cooker will automatically enter **KEEP WARM** mode. Press the CANCEL button and allow the cooker to naturally depressurize for 5-10 minutes. Then carefully release the remaining pressure manually and open the lid.
6. Remove the pears from the cooker to a bowl using a slotted spoon.
7. Turn the cooker off (disconnect the cooker from power source) and let the syrup in it thicken a little bit.
8. Drizzle the syrup over the pears and serve with fresh berries.

Day 28 – Raspberry Raisin Bread Pudding

Servings: 6

Ingredients:

- 4 large eggs, whisked
- 2 cups unsweetened coconut milk
- ½ cup coconut sugar
- 1 teaspoon vanilla extract
- 3 cups cubed cinnamon raisin bread
- 1 cup fresh raspberries

Instructions:

1. Pour 2 cups of water into your Power Pressure Cooker XL.
2. In a medium mixing bowl, whisk together the eggs, coconut milk, coconut sugar, and vanilla extract.
3. Grease a soufflé dish that fits into your pressure cooker with cooking spray.

4. Combine the bread cubes and raspberries in the soufflé dish, spreading them evenly.
5. Pour in the whisked egg mixture and cover the dish with foil.
6. Close the lid and the pressure valve then cook for 25 minutes. To get 25 minutes cook time, you can press the SOUP/STEW button and then use the TIME ADJUSTMENT button to adjust to 25 minutes.
7. After the timer reaches 0, the cooker will automatically enter **KEEP WARM** mode. Press the CANCEL button and allow the cooker to naturally depressurize for 5-10 minutes. Then carefully release the remaining pressure manually and open the lid.
8. Remove the soufflé dish.
9. Cool the bread pudding on a wire rack for 15 to 20 minutes then serve warm.

Day 29 – Fluffy Chocolate Cake

Servings: 8 to 10

Ingredients:

- 1 ½ cups white cake flour
- ¼ cup unsweetened cocoa powder
- ¾ teaspoons baking powder
- Pinch of salt
- 2 large eggs, whisked
- ¾ cups white sugar
- 2 tablespoons melted coconut oil
- ¾ cups unsweetened coconut milk

Instructions:

1. Use a sifter to combine the flour, cocoa powder, baking powder and salt.
2. In a mixing bowl, beat together the eggs and the sugar.

3. Beat in the melted coconut oil then fold in the flour mixture.
4. Whisk in the coconut milk, using only as much as you need to wet the batter and make it smooth.
5. Grease a round cake pan with cooking spray then pour in the batter.
6. Place a steamer tray in your Power Pressure Cooker XL and pour in 1 cup of water.
7. Put the cake pan on top of the steamer tray then close the lid.
8. Close the lid and the pressure valve then cook for 30 minutes. To get 30 minutes cook time, you can press the FISH/VEGETABLES/STEAM button and then use the TIME ADJUSTMENT button to adjust to 30 minutes.
9. After the timer reaches 0, the cooker will automatically enter **KEEP WARM** mode. Press the CANCEL button and allow the cooker to naturally depressurize for 5-10 minutes. Then carefully release the remaining pressure manually and open the lid.
10. Allow the cake to cool completely before you take it out of the cooker.

Day 30 – Lemon Cheesecake with Berries

Servings:

Ingredients:

- 10 whole graham crackers
- 2/3 cups plus ½ tablespoon sugar
- ¼ cup melted coconut oil
- 2 tablespoons cornstarch
- Pinch of salt
- 2 (8-ounce) packages reduced fat cream cheese
- ½ cup light sour cream
- 2 tablespoons fresh lemon zest
- 1 teaspoon lemon extract
- 1 ½ cups fresh berries

Instructions:

1. Pulse the graham crackers in a food processor until they are finely ground then stir in ½ tablespoon of sugar.
2. Pour the mixture into a small bowl then stir in the melted coconut oil.
3. Line a cheesecake pan with parchment then press the cracker crumb mixture into the bottom to form the crust.
4. Bake the crust at 325°F for 15 minutes then set aside to cool.
5. Combine the rest of the sugar in a mixing bowl with the cornstarch and salt.
6. In another bowl, beat together the cream cheese and sugar mixture until it is thick and creamy.
7. Add the sour cream, lemon zest and lemon extract then beat until combined.
8. Beat in the eggs one at a time then pour the mixture into the cheesecake pan.
9. Place a steamer tray in your Power Pressure Cooker XL then pour in 1 cup of water.
10. Put the cheesecake pan on top of the steamer tray then close the lid and the pressure valve.
11. Cook the cheesecake for 25 minutes. To get 25-minutes cook time, press the Fish/Veg./Steam button and then use the TIME ADJUSTMENT button to adjust to 25 minutes.
12. After the timer reaches 0, the cooker will automatically enter **KEEP WARM** mode. Press the CANCEL button and allow the cooker to naturally depressurize for 5-10 minutes. Then carefully release the remaining pressure manually and open the lid.

13. Remove the cheesecake and let it cool to room temperature.
14. Chill the cheesecake for several hours then top with fresh berries to serve.

Just Before You Go…(Please Read!)

What you eat really affect your life and that is why you need to really watch what you are taking into your body. Interestingly, there are cheap quality food items that you can include in your diet if you are serious about improving your health. You can visit http://pharmibrahim.blogspot.com/2017/02/recommended-food-items.html to check them out.